The AAA Way to Fundraising Success:

Maximum Involvement, Maximum Results

Published by
•
Whit Press
4701 SW Admiral Way, #125
Seattle, WA 98116
•
PO Box 13275 / mail
252 E Pearl / ship
Jackson WY 83002
•
www.whitpress.org
•
ISBN 978-0-9720205-9-6
Library of Congress Control Number:
2009933017

Whit Press books are made possible in major part by the generous support of
Nancy Nordhoff, Kate Nelson, Margot Snowdon, Lynn Garvey, Kerri Ballard,
our individual contributors and the following organizations:

• The Seattle Foundation
• Seattle Office of Arts & Cultural Affairs
• The Breneman-Jaech Foundation
• Hill-Snowdon Foundation

For you all, our most heartfelt thanks and gratitude.

FOREWORD

In the philanthropic sector, we are seekers of change, solutions, innovation and community impact. As brokers of community dreams, we long to see a world altered through our efforts. And yet we are continually stymied by the challenge of engaging board members in helping us create the resources and relationships that will fund those dreams. We try, often in vain, to get our board members actively involved in fund raising. But, increasingly, we are realizing that the traditional approaches to philanthropic engagement may not work with the new generations of volunteers and donor-investors. As they join our boards, we see this with discomfiting clarity.

21st Century philanthropic growth has brought new opportunities, however, for rethinking how we involve community leaders in our work. An increasing number of the new board members — whether Millennials or recently-retired (many now in "encore career") Baby Boomers — want to be involved in new ways.

They are hands-on. They are busy. They want specific assignments. They like tasks that don't take a long time but have high impact. Committees, to them, are passé: they would rather be on a time-limited task force or off on an assignment that excites them — often one of their own choosing, using their technology-based social networks or their personal circle of friends.

They also want to know that you know what makes them tick and why they are involved. They want to do what they want to do. Their passion is evident but its source is not always obvious. They are impatient with the process-driven nature of traditional board governance and fundraising, and they want action. Sitting with their Blackberries or iPhones in their hands texting just under the edge of the board room table, and their mobile phones on "vibrate" on top of the table, they are ever-connected with a world that holds our future: their social networks, their families, their work.

They want to be involved not just with fund raising, finance or administration — they want to get close to the program. They want to offer insights and solutions. They want to work with an entire staff that is engaged in a philanthropic vision for the community — not in organizations where development and the board's support of it is an operation separate from the rest of the organization.

- AAA is a new way to involve your board members. It is not an "add on" to what they are already doing. It is a way of organizing and managing what you have already identified as priorities in your strategic or development plan. AAA offers board members and other volunteers the opportunity to self-select tasks they would like to do within the roles of Ambassador, Advocate and Asker.

- AAA provides a way to find out what makes our volunteers tick — including those new to philanthropy and those needing to renew their commitment. By offering people the opportunity to say how they want to be involved, we ignite their imaginations about their possible role in philanthropy and the results they can produce.

- AAA offers a way to embrace not only this new generation of leadership, but the generations that have served us so well over decades of vibrant philanthropy. While the engagement of a 30-something may be different from the engagement of a 70-something, the honor we give to both by linking them with tasks that are motivating, gratifying and successful has the same result: an ever-increasing commitment to serve the organization.

- AAA is an innovation in board organization and motivation. It influences the tone of board meetings and the intensity of a board member's engagement. It dignifies every step in the development process, and lets everyone feel a part of your success.

It is a framework for reporting philanthropic activity and a solution to problems of board engagement and enthusiasm. It works. It has brought success to increasing numbers of organizations. It is practical, appropriate and flexible.

Creating a AAA board just might change your board members' involvement. And encourage staff involvement. And that could change your organization's future.

Give it a try.

Kay Sprinkel Grace

CONTENTS

The AAA Way to Fundraising Success:

Maximum Involvement, Maximum Results

Kay Sprinkel Grace

Whit Press

Seattle, Washington • Jackson Hole, Wyoming • www.whitpress.org

INTRODUCTION

When I work with boards, we always get around to discussing the issue of fund raising. I ask, "How many of you really like asking for money?" On a great day, one-third of the hands will go up. On an average day, one-fourth or less. On too many days, two or three. The others groan, smile with embarrassment and then tell me why they don't like to ask for money.

"Fear of rejection."
"Feels like begging."
"The quid pro quo problem."

Although the reasons are understandable, they beg the question. Boards are responsible for raising money. If only one-third or a handful are willing to ask, what roles do the other board members play? How do you create a cohesive fundraising team? How do you get everyone on your board engaged in developing donors and funds for your organization?

Whether you are board chair, board member, development committee chair or development director, this book is for you. It tells you how to create and implement a program that will engage everyone on your board in donor and fund development. The principle is simple: when people are engaged in your fundraising program in ways that tap into their motivation and build their confidence, they succeed and stay involved.

Imagine a future where everyone on your board is willing to get involved in raising money. Where everyone has an assignment — and does it. If you dream of such a board, read on — but with one condition: you have to abandon the idea that everyone on your board or volunteer committee is going to ask for money. That simply has not worked in my experience. Fortunately, there are many other important fund development roles board members can play.

The Triple A Program

AAA stands for Ambassador, Advocate and Asker.

Each of the AAA roles organizes relationship development and fundraising tasks around individual volunteer motivation. Each role offers multiple opportunities for involvement. Some people sign up for tasks in all three roles. Others choose just the first two, and still others want only to be Ambassadors.

AAA boards are those where board members are offered opportunities to select from multiple assignments, drawn from the strategic and/or development plan(s), that fall into the AAA categories. The organization follows through by guiding and monitoring the board members' chosen assignments. Because board members can sign up for the things they like to do, the likelihood of them completing their assignments greatly increases. All AAA options support the on-going development, fund raising, community outreach, program support and donor/board member recruitment responsibilities of board members — and the strategic plan of the organization.

A "Triple A" organization is one where the quality and results of board engagement in donor development and fundraising advance not only what the organization wants to accomplish, but also the board members' feeling of success and satisfaction.

I have worked with thousands of Ambassadors, a few of whose stories are told in this book. I have also worked with extraordinary Advocates who formally (with the planning commission, Congress or town council) or informally (on the golf course or at lunch) are able to state the case for support and engage others in a dialog that lays the path for Askers to do their work more effectively. And I have worked with impressive Askers, who do it so effortlessly and so engagingly that while they are closing the gift they are opening the doors to a long and beneficial relationship between the donor and the organization.

The AAA approach, which comes out of my experience as a volunteer leader, a development officer and now a consultant, allows board and non-board development volunteers to see the array of roles available and the tasks they can perform. When the pressure to "just get out there and ask" is removed as an inclusive directive for all board members, they become valued, energetic and enthused members of your development team.

Kay Sprinkel Grace

Chapter 1:

Why AAA Works

People are motivated, or they wouldn't join our boards. So when they don't get involved, or don't do what we hope they will do, we are probably not engaging them around their motivation. Once we know what motivates a volunteer, we can offer opportunities for engagement around that motivation and get great results.

Motivation increases when we uncover a volunteer's "confidence zone:" assignments that encourage confidence in their skills, the organization and their potential for success. So why is it, when we are thinking about ways to engage our volunteers in fund development, that we approach them with a list of what we want them to do, rather than finding out what they want or like to do?

No wonder so many volunteers feel reluctant about fundraising. In most cases, they are not asked what they like to do, and they are not motivated by the tasks we assign them. Many of them are very apprehensive about asking for money. Assignments languish. Their intentions are good, but they simply cannot ask.

While you may be one who is willing (and even eager) to be both a partner and leader in asking, the majority of board members and other fundraising volunteers feel more confident when we offer opportunities for involvement in resource development that do not require asking directly for money.

Increasing Board Involvement

As a leader or board member, the most important thing you can do to increase the involvement of others in fundraising is to listen to board members as they tell you about the activities they enjoy and are willing to do. Then you can connect them with a wide choice of important "development" tasks that match those interests.

To make this work, adjust your expectations. Attach respect and a sense of importance to assignments that don't involve asking for money. Equalize the recognition among those who make friends (Ambassadors), those who make your case either informally or formally in the community (Advocates) and those who do the actual asking (Askers). Activities of Ambassadors, Advocates and Askers are interdependent functions, but each requires a particular kind of interest, aptitude and recognition for success.

Transforming Power of AAA

The AAA program can transform your board and your organization.

I have seen this program change the way people feel about their board experience and how they recruit others. In several organizations, it has become the basis for a new vocabulary when talking about board activities. In others, board members who previously were apologetic because they could not (or would not) ask for money were gratified when people they connected with in the community entered into long term donor-investor relationships with the organization.

I have witnessed the appreciation CEOs extend to volunteers who advocate publicly for their organization or for an issue that is critical to their future. And I have seen volunteer Askers marvel at how easy it was to close on a gift because an Ambassador's cultivation efforts built a strong connection with the prospect.

Because people feel good about what they are doing, they do it. That's what AAA is all about. The reality of board service is that everyone needs to be involved in financial resource development. And yet, year after year, as revealed in studies and experience, it is the aspect of board service that concerns board and staff the most.

Although the AAA program initially was created for boards, some organizations are also using it for non-board fund development volunteers (major giving committees, regional committees of state or national organizations, e.g.). Still others have extended certain of the roles (Ambassador, Advocate) to non-development staff (program directors, financial and human resources officers, e.g.). The principles are the same, although the rules for engagement may differ.

AAA is a simple program to explain and to implement. It is not an "add on" to what you are already doing: it is a system for organizing and managing those tasks. It requires no special staffing, just willingness on the part of board and other volunteer leadership — and the staff that support them — to create, offer and monitor tasks that come out of existing development plans and tap into volunteer motivation.

Once up and running, AAA inspires new levels of achievement and shared satisfaction.

Chapter 2

AAA and Human Dynamics at Play

In my work with boards, I observe two levels of motivation in most board members:

1. deep program-related motivation (mission, vision and values)
2. immediate and more personal motivation (other people on the board, community recognition, professional or personal growth).

Whether fellow board member, board leader or staff, your job is to intensify their deeper motivation (it fans their passion) by offering them the most positive volunteer experience possible. When people feel good about their success, they feel good about the organization. They grow into champions.

Find the Right Fundraising Role

Find the right fundraising role for each board member. When board members are assigned to tasks in fundraising that they are uncomfortable doing, their overall motivation for getting and staying engaged with us diminishes. They begin to dread (and avoid) involvement. They may stop coming to meetings. They lose passion for the program because they feel guilty (or overwhelmed) relative to what we are asking them to do. When we listen to what they enjoy doing, and match it to the things we want done, their energy soars.

When we recruit volunteers, we hope to connect with their values and inspire them with ours. Enlistment usually includes meetings and an orientation to familiarize the candidate with the organization. We review the basics of board or committee membership. We want to make sure they know what we expect.

But do we also discuss with them how they like to be involved in fundraising? Do we ask them about their fundraising experience? Do we find out the kinds of things they have done and what they would like to do? Or do we make assumptions that, if they previously were on the board of the symphony (known to be a "fundraising board") that they are seasoned, motivated fund raisers? Or, worse, do we lay out our expectations of board involvement in fundraising in a way that is immediately burdensome to them ("We expect each board member to bring in $2500 a year in addition to his or her own gift, and to sell or buy at least one table for $5,000 at our annual auction")? While this may work for volunteers in some organizations, for many it simply does not.

Origins of AAA

The seed for AAA came out of my own experience as a volunteer overseeing the recruitment of nearly 2000 volunteers for a personal solicitation program for a major university campaign. When we called them, instead of telling them about our program and what we wanted them to do, we started by thanking them for their previous volunteer work for the university (or in their community) and then asked them to talk about the fundraising activities they had most enjoyed. We did not mention the program we were representing, just the overall campaign.

From their responses ("I couldn't possibly ask for money, but I am happy to entertain prospects in my home," or "I prefer just to write notes on letters," or "I love to meet other alumni and engage them in a personal ask,") we made program assignments that resulted in an incredibly high volunteer retention throughout the five years of the campaign. We knew what we wanted done (cultivation, personal solicitation, stewardship) and were able to make assignments within our program that were satisfying to the volunteers. Those we felt would not be motivated by our array of assignments were referred to another program of the campaign more suited to their preferred activities.

Adults will to tell you what they do and do not like to do. You don't have to guess or hope. When we listen, we can match what we hear with tasks that need to be done.

The following chapters describe each AAA role. When reading, think of those on your board who are already Ambassadors, Advocates or Askers. Read this with your development plan by your side, and think of the tasks in your development plan that they could do. You'll see later how these tasks will fall into the AAA categories. That will provide the platform for creating your checklist (Chapter 6) and implementing the program.

Chapter 3:

AMBASSADORS— Making Friends

The tasks for each of the AAA roles are drawn from your development plan and are tailored for your organization. Your board members will select the tasks in each category they would like to do.

The following information gives you examples of the Ambassador role which you can use when categorizing the tasks from your plan to include in your AAA survey and the orientation to the program you will do for your board. An overview of the tasks for Advocates and Askers follows in Chapters 3 and 4.

Being an Ambassador

An Ambassador makes friends. An Ambassador is a key player in values-based relationship-building, the foundation of successful fund raising. Although your Ambassadors may seldom or never ask for a gift, they are critically important to your fund development efforts. We are daily reminded that fundraising is not about money, it is about relationships.

Everyone on your board should be willing to be an Ambassador — if they are not willing to make friends for the organization, they should not be on the board. They will make friends in the traditional ways, and in the new media ways: your younger board members "friends" may be the networks they have created on My Space or Facebook — but they will be willing, I have found, to import your "widget" into their emails for the purpose of letting others know about your organization.

Ambassador Extraordinaire

In 1995 I consulted with the American Library in Paris on a small capital campaign. My first job was to engage board members in the campaign. There was little tradition of board involvement in resource development at the Library, and I seized on the slightest offer of help. One of the board members was very involved with an array of French-American organizations in Paris. She said she would be happy to get together and was willing to do anything "but ask for money." So, I asked her how she would like to help. She responded that she had "great lists" and was willing to bring them for me to review.

"Great lists" was perhaps the philanthropic understatement of the late 20th Century. In more than 25 years of living back and forth between Paris and the US, she had made more friends for French-American organizations, including the Library, than anyone else I met. Naturally amiable, and therefore often assigned to welcoming or orientation committees for new arrivals to Paris, she not only greeted newcomers, she became friends with many of them. Over the years, as people came and went on assignments that brought them to Paris for a year or five or 20, she kept in touch. And she kept notes. When these ex-pats moved back to the US, she continued sending them announcements about special events at the various French-American institutions — just in case a planned trip might coincide with one of them. On her annual summer stays in the US, she often visited with those she had gotten to know in Paris.

Her list reflected this information and her wise insights. The people she had maintained relationships with over the years became the basis for the first cultivation visits for the campaign. With her list as our guide, we called on individuals during a trip to the US to share the vision for an expanded American Library and assess their interest in supporting the campaign. They were delighted to meet with us, hear the plan and discuss a possible commitment to the campaign. And, they all added that they would not be meeting with us if it were not for the way in which their friend had kept them connected all these years. We received promises of some generous commitments, and when I returned to Paris a week later I called and asked if I could take her to lunch to report on our success. I told her that she had "most likely raised quite a bit of money" for the campaign. Surprised, she retorted, "But I don't raise money." My response: "Oh yes you do."

She was the consummate Ambassador.

Formalizing the Ambassador Role

Although making friends may be second nature, good Ambassadors still need to be oriented to their job and coached in the message. It will grow their confidence for the tasks they have selected to do.

As a first requirement, train your board members and other volunteers to give the "elevator speech" — the short summary of what you are doing, why it is essential, what the impact is/has been. They should also know how to ask the "elevator question" at the end of their speech: "You seem very interested. Is there other information I can offer?" or "In what I have just described, is there anything of particular interest?" or "I am delighted you are interested. We are having a (tour/event/open house) in the next few weeks — may I call you and tell you more about it? We would love for you to come." The ability to easily say the elevator speech and ask the elevator question is essential for the confidence of all Ambassadors.

Cultivation

Ambassadors are instrumental in donor cultivation. One woman I know who is a generous philanthropist but simply unwilling to ask for money opens her lovely home regularly to organizations with which she is involved, and hosts lunches or dinners so the organizations can cultivate and steward donors. Her connection with these organizations is reason enough for people to come to these events, and she enhances their ability to raise money. Other cultivation occurs at special events (see below) or at regularly scheduled on-site tours, talks or gatherings.

If they want to be involved in face-to-face cultivating, Ambassadors should be open to trying the "two ears/one mouth ratio" — asking open ended questions and listening actively for the answer.

- "Tell me how you first became interested in our concerts."
- "As you have heard the stories of some of the girls we have helped, what questions do you have?"
- "Your support of homeless organizations in our community is positively inspiring. What is it about our organization you would like to know?"

If Ambassadors listen well, the follow up questions will flow right out of the answers they hear. Ted Koppel always said that he asked for two or three questions from his producers for each "Nightline" interview. If the first question was good enough he never had to go to the other prepared questions.

He was guided in his next question by listening to the answer to the first.

Stewardship

In addition to their role as cultivators — building the relationships that make it easier for the Askers to do their job — Ambassadors can also be invited to become stewards. In a capital campaign, they are effective in making sure that those who make their gifts early in the campaign stay connected to the organization and the campaign throughout its long duration. They are particularly effective at keeping donors of planned gifts engaged — often uncovering the desire of the individual to make another kind of planned gift, or an outright gift.

Offer Ambassadors a role in your Thankathons for annual and capital donors at all levels, and as a follow up to special events. Although they will not connect with every donor they call, they can leave a message expressing gratitude. And, donors or attendees with whom they do connect will offer Ambassadors a one-to-one experience with delighted donors. One organization has people come in every other Saturday to telephone members and thank them. Recently, they have begun calling members just prior to the time they receive their annual renewal letter. The renewal rate is improving.

You can encourage Ambassadors to engage in the lost art of letter writing. Ask them if they would like to write thank you or impact update notes to donors whenever possible. If they complain their handwriting is terrible, assure them that people are so thrilled to get handwritten letters they won't mind if it is a challenge to read.

Social networking may be the way some of your board members want to "cultivate." Your organization may already have a social networking web-based program they can use or they may use their own resources on My Space, Twitter or Facebook. It is an Ambassador role.

As both cultivators and stewards, Ambassadors may also want to host tours of your facilities and make calls to encourage people to come to an event. Your best Ambassadors are sincerely interested in people, and all of your Ambassadors should be interested enough to keep the donor connected with your organization.

At Special Events

Ambassadors tend to be good listeners — they enjoy finding out more about people and their interests. When planning an event, offer a specific role to your best Ambassadors. If they are willing, be sure they have a list of people you would like them to talk with during the event. Give them some background on each (but remind them not to bring the background information to the event). Provide a special designation on the name tag of all board members and, for willing Ambassadors, an "Ask Me" button is a good idea at a large event. Give them plenty of background information on the venue, the purpose of the event and how the attendees can get more involved with your organization. Invite willing Ambassadors to circulate among the guests and provide welcoming words, directions or enough conversation to make people feel at home and to find out what some of their interests are.

When it's time, seat your donors and your board members strategically. A favorite cartoon shows an elegantly dressed woman putting out the place cards around a formally set dinner table: "Donor, Non-donor, Donor, Non-donor..." When board member Ambassadors engage prospective or current donors in conversation, you convey that your organization not only knows who they are but are interested in them.

After every event, be sure to have Ambassadors practice a routine of conveying information they have learned to the staff or board leaders at your organization. There are a number of ways to do this: a phone call the next day either from the volunteer to a staff person or to another volunteer, an email, or by using a quick form you can email to them or put on your board member's dedicated web site to be completed and returned. An easy information-gathering form is the Action Update found in the Appendix, Exhibit A. The value of the form is that it records the information in a standard way. Make sure all callers use the same form to organize information. Keep it a system that people can follow easily.

Getting information from the Ambassadors into the data base is critical for the eventual work of the Askers. Clarification of the information once received is often a very good way to connect Ambassadors and Askers in strategic planning for the solicitation. It provides Ambassadors with insights into the process, without requiring them to actually ask.

As Storytellers

Ambassadors are often great story-tellers, so refresh their supply of stories regularly. Jim Collins, in his monograph Good to Great and the Social Sector gives nonprofits a wonderful tip: because it is often difficult for us to quantify our results (how can we measure the way a concert changes a child's appreciation for music?) he encourages us to use stories. People remember stories when they support statistics ("Last year more than 400 4th Graders were able to attend our afternoon concerts supported by your gift — and they were very candid in their enthusiasm. One letter we received from a student tells the story better than I can….."). People will multiply that letter by 400 others that could have been written. When people hear the stories, they understand the impact.

Make sure your social networkers have stories they can post to their web sites.

Encouraging Your Best Ambassadors

While all of your board members and other key volunteers are potential Ambassadors, some will be better at it than others. As you think of tasks you can invite Ambassadors to do in your organization, be thinking also about who will be your best Ambassadors. Like the board member in France, good Ambassadors think ahead to the next opportunity to engage new or continuing constituencies in the organization. They are often the ones at board or committee meetings who say, "You know, I've been thinking about how we could increase attendance/reach out to that community/get more people to work at our annual event at the County Fair..." They are thinking about long term engagement.

And, when you implement the AAA and prepare your list of opportunities for board involvement, remember to keep the task list refreshed. Even the most enthusiastic Ambassador will be looking for some new things to do. Review your plan, and pull out more plums. Here are some tasks that might be motivating to some:

- To be in charge of an event.
- To create and lead a board member mentoring program for new members
- To reach out to new members, if yours is a membership organization
- To use their creative Ambassador energy to form a new support group (e.g., younger members, professional or geographical affinity groups, etc.).
- To work with you to create a cultivation program leading up to a capital, endowment or annual campaign.

Whatever they choose to do, meet with them as often as feasible to give them feedback and thank them. Make sure that at the yearly meeting you have with the board member, the board chair and the CEO, that their list of Ambassador activities and successes is reviewed and appreciated

Fundraising, we remember, is not about money: it is about

relationships. Ambassadors are the front line of relationship building. It will serve your organization well to organize, acknowledge and encourage everyone on your board to be an Ambassador, and to offer tasks that they will be motivated to do.

More will be said about rewards and recognition for Ambassadors in a later chapter. The most important thing to remember is that sometimes it is hard to remember who introduced or first engaged a person who ends up making a significant major or planned gift. Keep track of the trail. Honor the people willing to make connections for you. They are a key platform for your successful resource development.

They are your Ambassadors.

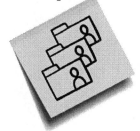

Chapter 4

ADVOCATES—
Making the Case

The simplest description of the Advocates' role is that they make the case. On a AAA survey, they choose from Advocate activities that are motivating to them: working with legislators, visiting a foundation to participate in a report, giving a speech to their Rotary Club, taking a position on an issue or program on their social networking site, or sounding out a potential board member while golfing.

Informal Advocacy
Informal advocacy takes place in the car pool, on the Internet, on the golf course or at a social event. The Advocates' role differs from that of the Ambassadors because, even in informal situations, they have been coached to plant seeds of interest or future action in those people your organization wants to engage. Advocates are coached to say or listen for certain things.

- Would their friend be interested in coming on the board at some future time?

- Do they think the firing of the CEO has had a negative effect on this individual and others in the community?
- Might they be interested in learning more about an outreach project the organization is considering?

Informal advocacy requires Advocates to advance ideas and listen to the reaction — and then to report back to board or staff leadership. The Action Update form offered in Appendix A works well for Advocates, too — the difference is that the report will include answers to specific questions the organization has asked the Advocate to raise.

Formal Advocacy

From time to time, all organizations need friends in city hall, the state legislature, Congress or the national office of your local affiliate. You may also ask board members to do an email "blast" to their address book on an issue that is critical to your future. That's when Advocates may be asked to provide formal advocacy. For some people on your board this is a highly motivating task, and they will offer to do it so they exercise their experience and connections in a way that brings them a sense of pride, power and accomplishment.

There are people on your board who will be very motivated to send emails, make a phone call or personal appearance during hearings, public sessions or other times when your organization needs a citizen's voice. Many board members of public television stations across America enthusiastically participate in what is known as "Capitol Hill Days" every February — traveling to Washington, DC, to meet with their Congressional Representatives and Senators to let them know how important public television is in their communities. They are exercising an Advocacy role. So are board members who represent your organization officially at an inauguration, graduation or other ceremony or volunteer to participate in your Speakers' Bureau.

Although public speaking may not be every Advocate's primary strength, utilize the talents of willing and gifted speaker-Advocates at service clubs, churches and other gatherings. Provide your speakers with basic talking points including the key ideas from your case, some statistics and illustrative stories, and ask to review the first speech before it is delivered. It is a good idea for someone from the organization's leadership to attend the first talk that your speakers give — you will want to know what is being said on your behalf and how it was received. Over time, you should develop enough confidence in your Advocate-speakers that continued review and attendance is not necessary.

What Advocates Need for Confidence and Success

Whether formal or informal, Advocates need more than just a nice story to tell. The entire board should go through a training session in donor and fund development principles and strategies, even though not all of them will be Askers. Ambassadors will understand the way they lead the process, and Advocates will find themselves using many of the Askers' tools.

Like Askers, Advocates need to know how to present the case and be very well coached in handling objections and answering tough questions. They should be very clear about what the organization expects as an outcome of the conversation or public appearance: information about what steps to take next, action on an issue that is critical to your planning or activities, or people with whom you should speak next.

What Advocates Can Do

While all board members and other volunteers bring their community connections to your organization, Advocates are offered opportunities to be more intentional with their connections. Their work or community experience may have put them into the active circle of opinion, thought, social or political leadership in your community. It gives them pleasure to exercise these connections on your behalf IF you have given them the training and information they need be effective.

In one small organization that provided after school tutoring programs, there was a growing need for more school sites in particular neighborhoods. One of the board members — who had some political ambition and was eyeing an eventual seat on the school board — turned out to have connections at the school district that no one else had. Within months three new sites had been secured, thanks to his efforts in presenting the case for program expansion.

In another example, an organization created community controversy over its determination to demolish an earthquake-damaged building to create a more accessible, beautiful and functional facility. The damaged building was original to the site, historic in terms of age although not in significance, and had many defenders. Even when presented with letters from the long-deceased architect, attesting to the temporary nature of the building's construction and site placement and conveying a larger vision for the complex, the planning commission still heard fervent arguments from those who wished it preserved. For months, permission to demolish was withheld. In meeting after meeting, a dozen or more supporters of the new architectural vision spoke to the planning commission — or just showed up and sat silently — testifying to the importance of demolition and rebuilding. In the end, it was the persistence and numbers of the organization's Advocates that won the day. The damaged building was demolished, the vision was fulfilled with the new building complex, and the site now stands as one of that city's most beautiful and important landmarks.

Other Roles for Advocates
Another role Advocates enjoy is board recruitment. Many Advocates have a knack for putting a fine point on the key issues and opportunities your organization offers to potential board members. Engage them as leaders on this committee

along with a few Ambassadors, and maybe even a few Askers. They make a good team.

Advocates are often from professions (law, accounting, consulting) where they have been trained to get quickly to the purpose of a meeting, summarize their arguments succinctly, and not take too much time to convey their ideas. This works well for them as Advocates because the time they have with a legislator — or in the car pool — is limited. Be sure to equip your Advocates with the facts they need to present, the stories to support those facts, the outcomes you anticipate, responses to objections they may encounter, and the expectations you have for next steps or delivery of information.

Just as it is important to remember that an Ambassador may have been the initial link with a person who recently made a major gift, be sure to recognize the work of your Advocates in moving your mission, vision and agenda in the community. Often behind the scenes, Advocates may not get the recognition and gratitude that Askers get. This is particularly true with board members who are working their social networks on your behalf. Make sure that Advocates are acknowledged for their successes. Offer them appropriate recognition for raising awareness of your organization, recruiting board members, forging a collaborative partnership with another nonprofit, making the case with a legislator or city council member or successfully moving a reluctant funder into a position where an Asker was able to succeed in getting the gift.

A major trend in 21st century philanthropy is the desire our communities have for us to work with other similar organizations. Advocates may have skills in negotiating partnerships or collaborations. When they are coached in the purpose and outcomes of their assignments they can become champions of visionary compromise in working for the best possible organizational and/or resource alignment.
In 2006, in northeastern Ohio, eight land trusts merged to

become Western Reserve Land Conservancy (WRLC) — a regional entity that aims to protect forests, farms, wetlands and other natural areas in a 14-county area along the shores of Lake Erie. In their press release announcing the merger, an unknown source was quoted as saying, "It's easier to put a man on the moon than to merge nonprofits."

Lauri Gross, media relations staffer with WRLC, who called me with this story because she had heard about AAA, cited the Advocacy role of board members of several these organizations as extremely valuable in effecting the merger. According to the press release, they saw that it "was about the land" and that a merged organization would ultimately have more leveraging power and be more effective.

Most Advocates are also great Ambassadors, and some will even be Askers. As Advocates, they work well for us both behind the scenes and in leadership roles in the community.

Think carefully about the many ways you can invite Advocates to be involved on your behalf and add those tasks to the checklist in Chapter 6 as you develop it.

Chapter 5:

ASKERS—
Making the Ask

In the minds of many, this role is the most important one in resource development. It is also the role we used to believe everyone should be willing and able to do. We all wanted "fundraising boards" — a designation that clearly leads to a limited candidate pool!

In reality, just one-quarter to one-third of the members of most boards are willing to become Askers. The reasons for this are well known: too much has been written about why people don't want to ask to give it space here. Treasure the Askers you have, use the information in this chapter to increase your understanding of Askers and what they need, and use the confidence-building found for many in the Ambassador and Advocate experience to help increase your Asker ranks.

Tasks for Askers
We all think we know what Askers do. Their work is pretty straightforward. We can start with the premise that they are people who enjoy asking. But any discussion of Askers

should start by defining what we mean by "asking." This becomes very important when preparing the checklist that board members will use to indicate how they want to be involved.

Be sure to offer the full range of asking activities so you can uncover the widest range of volunteer interest and motivation. Let them know that asking includes writing personal letters, embedding a link to your web site into their emails and sending that out to their friends, making personal phone calls, as well as making personal visits. Offer them opportunities to accompany fellow board members or non-board volunteers or staff members on a call until they become more confident. People are more apt to sign up as Askers if they see several confidence-zone choices in tasks. If they think asking means only face to face, with no options, they may decline. You may lose someone who would love to ask someone in a different way.

Board members will tell you what kinds of asks they are willing to make. When you meet with them to review their completed AAA checklist (Chapter 6), find out more.

- If they want to write personal letters, how can you help them?
- What do they need from the organization to set up a technology-based ask using their own social networks?
- If they will make personal phone calls, will they be from your lists or from theirs? If from theirs, provide guidelines for clearing those names so that others are not asking the same people.

If they want to accompany another volunteer or staff person on a call or feel they are ready to initiate a face to face ask, gauge how skilled they are at this by asking them to tell you about a time when they did this for your organization or another.

Find out what inspires them about your organization, and what they think their talking points will be.

By further exploring the things that motivate them, you will gain additional insights that will help you in working with them.

Many Askers are also willing to be Ambassadors and some will be Advocates, too. Those who sign up for the full AAA are going to be the leaders for your development efforts.

Characteristics of Askers

Sometimes a new board member or committee volunteer will seem like he or she is going to be a "natural asker." I am not sure I could describe that person, because in my decades of work as a volunteer and professional I have seen successful askers whose styles and approach varied widely. Extrovert or introvert, amiable or analytical, funny or somber — as long as the style is genuinely theirs, it works. Style is incidental to integrity, clarity, connection with the prospect and passion for the cause. Sometimes the people we think will be least effective turn out to be the best Askers, and I know people who seem like "naturals" who love to schmooze but cannot close when asking for a gift.

What are the some of the characteristics of successful Askers? These are the things I have found to be consistent, regardless of individual style.

They are:
- Good listeners.
- Empathetic.
- Donor-focused.
- Willing to be trained and coached even if they have lots of asking experience.
- Confident about the organization's reputation and future and in their own ability to handle objections or surprises and to close the ask.

- Enthused about your organization and able to talk about its impact in your community.
- Supportive of the board and administration when they talk with others (screen your Askers to make sure none of them are people with issues about your organization or its leaders — you want them to have confidence in your organization as well as themselves).

Building Asker Confidence

Be sure you assign your best staff or board leadership to support your Askers, especially those who are willing to make personal face-to-face asks.

All of the AAA roles need tools, techniques and support to be successful — but the Askers must be especially well-prepared, supported and equipped. For the Asker — no matter what approach they are going to use — there needs to be strong guidance, continuity and responsiveness to requests. For no other role do you need such a high level of reliability, responsiveness and know-how from staff or other leaders. Here are some things you can do to help them be more successful.

- Make sure they are well informed and well trained not just in asking but in asking for your organization (know the facts, the stories, the programs and the mission).
- Be sure they can handle tough questions and objections.
- Match them with prospective or current donors with whom they have the highest potential for success.
- Team them with another board asker or staff leader.
- Using staff or volunteer leadership, organize

the logistics of the Ask (prospect information, amount to ask for, purpose of the gift, setting for the meeting, case points to emphasize, etc.) so the Asker's focus can be on the single purpose of getting (or renewing) the gift and ensuring that the meeting is the beginning (or continuation) of a relationship, not just a transaction.

- Explain the cultivation and outreach that has been done with the prospect so far, letting them know how they have benefited from the work of Ambassadors and Advocates who have been involved in the relationship building.

Askers are motivated by success. While the impact of Ambassadors and Advocates may require weeks, months or years to see, very often an Asker gets an answer immediately.

If it is negative, it can diminish motivation and enthusiasm. When launching Askers with their first assignments, try to offer them a "mixed portfolio" of no more than five prospects — two or three who you know will give generously and enthusiastically and immediately, and two or three who will take a little more time and present a few more challenges. Encourage the Askers to start with the ones who are ready to give. It will build confidence and give them practice for the later, more difficult asks.

This little story is about a phenomenal Asker who, in the course of her volunteer role in a capital campaign, worked with a mixed portfolio, had astounding success, and deftly employed her skills as an Ambassador as well.

The volunteer, a young woman who had stepped down from her demanding job in the investment world to be a stay-at-home mother for two small children, suddenly realized she craved adult company. She said yes to the recruitment call and volunteered to make as many calls as we wanted her to.

Although we assigned her only five at a time, she completed them all with energy, engagement and success, and at the end of the campaign she had completed more than 30 calls on behalf of the campaign, most of them successful asks for $10,000 to $100,000. One of those asks brought in a seven-figure gift — significantly larger than those expected from her area of the campaign.

Among her assignments was a man nearly 60 years her senior who, she found from his wife, was terminally ill. Although she never spoke with him directly, she built a caring relationship with the man's wife, entirely over the phone. Over the course of two years, the volunteer would call occasionally to see how the man was doing. Towards the end of the campaign, he died. The volunteer expressed her sympathy to the wife and daughter, and was moved when they asked to meet her to talk about a gift in his memory. Thinking it would be for the amount that had been suggested in her assignment, she was surprised to learn they were thinking not of a gift of $10,000, but of a gift in excess of $1 million. Repeatedly, the wife spoke of how much the volunteer's follow up had meant, inspiring her to speak with her husband to determine his intent.

That campaign occurred more than 20 years ago, and the volunteer was recognized with a special award at the campaign's conclusion. And, she continues to ask. She was recently recognized by her university for her success as an Asker in yet another campaign.

Some people just love asking.

Keeping Askers Motivated

Be sensitive to the needs of your Askers for feedback and reinforcement. We know that people volunteer for many reasons that have nothing to do with your organization — they have their own needs for skills acquisition, affiliation with people who share their values, a diversion from a demanding career, respite from the draining home situation, an opportunity to be recognized in the community as a good citizen or other personal and sometimes professional reasons. Although the goal of engaging them as Askers is to increase your organization's development and fundraising success, don't forget to give the kind of feedback and encouragement that is geared to what you know they are seeking in their volunteer experience.

As Askers accrue successes, acknowledge them as they wish to be recognized: at a board or committee meeting or with a personal note or phone call. Ultimately, for each of the AAA volunteer roles, it is the success of your entire development program that should be the greatest motivation of all.

Encourage your Askers to tell their stories at board and committee meetings. Inside every Ambassador and Advocate an Asker is hiding — just waiting for the right moment or encouragement to break through the fear or anxiety that holds them back. When Askers tell their stories of success (and failure) at meetings, others listen. They begin to see themselves in these stories. They are thinking, "I could do that." Or, "I know that person, too — I could have done that." Candid, vulnerable stories from Askers will inspire others to tap into a latent motivation: to build on their experience as Ambassadors and/or Advocates and to perhaps at some point become an Asker.

Most volunteer organizations need and want more Askers. If you are chronically short of Askers, assemble donor development teams with all three roles represented. Because many Ambassadors and Advocates are uncomfortable with asking but are willing to do outreach, creating teams that engage all three A's can ultimately grow your number of Askers.

At one community college foundation, an Ambassador who had become a superb steward to the college's donors increasingly found herself with donors whose experience was so positive they wanted to make another gift. Teamed with Askers from her board, who did not know the donors as she did, on several occasions she found herself being the one to ask for the gift. Finally, she gave in to it. At a board meeting she confessed that she actually liked asking, after years of protesting that she would not (and could not) ask for money.

In a recent AAA implementation, it was a pleasant surprise to review the completed checklists. Board members, after several opportunities to learn about AAA and the variety of opportunities it offered for involvement, responded to the survey in this way: of the 21 board members, 13 indicated they would be AAA, 7 indicated they would be AA (not Askers) and one member indicated an interest in being an Ambassador only. This grid summary is Appendix B.

When organizations develop each of the AAA roles, offer thoughtful assignments, and focus on their interdependence, the likelihood for increasing the number of Askers will grow.

CHAPTER 6:

Putting AAA into Action

Introducing the Program to Your Board

The ease with which this program can be implemented was a surprise, even to me. Invited to facilitate the annual retreat for board and staff from the foundations of a large hospital system, I introduced the basic AAA program as a potential tool for increasing board engagement. It was not the focus of the retreat, just an aspect. In truth, I had not fully developed the materials or process.

The following year, invited to facilitate their retreat again, the organizers said that one of the foundations wanted time on the agenda to talk about their success with AAA. I was astonished to find they had already implemented the program. Their story was a delight to hear.

The board chair and foundation CEO had used the previous year's retreat power point and printed materials to give an orientation to their board about AAA, got their buy-in, worked with the sample checklist to tailor it for their foundation, and offered assignments based on the checklist. It had given them a tool for follow up with board members, had provided clarity to board members about expectations, and they were now using it as a basis for board recruitment. But it was the "unintended consequence" that really got my attention. They reported that some Ambassadors and Advocates had moved into the Asker role once they became confident with the role(s) for which they had signed up initially.

Before you can implement the AAA program, you need to know what needs to be done. Only when you have a strong sense of the most important tasks — and can link them to AAA roles — will volunteers feel as though what they sign up to do is truly important.

In one public television station, we structured the introduction of AAA in a novel way that I have recommended numerous times since. After the introduction of each of the three roles at the annual board retreat, the CEO singled out individuals on the board who were already playing that particular AAA role. He appreciated Ambassadors who had introduced him to people who were now major donors or who had hosted tours or events for the station. He identified the Advocates, and acknowledged one in particular who had successfully made the case to leaders she knew at the university medical school for collaborating with the station on a health series. And he identified others who, in their roles as Askers, had significantly increased the station's major gifts revenue.

This approach fulfilled one of the principles of this program: that it is not an add-on, it is a way of organizing what you are already doing. The board welcomed the program. Recently, to mark a full year of AAA, the CEO asked me to prepare a list of questions for them to discuss at their retreat. You will find those questions in Chapter 14.

Creating the AAA Survey
The survey tasks come from your strategic institutional and/or

development plan. If you don't have one, you will have to be more resourceful about identifying tasks — and AAA may inspire you to develop one.

Generating the checklist offers a great opportunity for board leaders and development staff to work together to identify the areas where volunteer involvement could make a big difference. It is best to brainstorm all possible activities — and then to assign them as Ambassador, Advocate or Asker functions.

Because AAA is not just about fund raising, but about all the things board members can do to grow relationships and visibility for the organization, the survey can include tasks like board recruitment, marketing and community outreach. The process allows us to think broadly about the entire continuum of development — from understanding program (the basis for the elevator speech and question) to marketing (what are the messages we send?) to community outreach (with what other agencies can we collaborate to extend our mission and how can volunteers help us bring in new constituencies?) to board recruitment (how can we engage board members who represent new community connections?) to the more traditional activities of cultivating potential donors, asking for gifts and maintaining good relationships with existing donors. The basic question is, "What needs to be done in order for us to achieve our fund development goals?"

Here is a sample list of activities. Take a look at it and think how you can use it as a springboard for creating your own list of opportunities. Then think about who on your board matches each of the "A" roles and what some of them are already doing. Return to the list, work with your own development plan, categorize it more carefully and make it a useful tool for you and your volunteers. The survey is also repeated in Appendix C.

AAA Board/Volunteer Program Survey
(See also Appendix A)
Sample Checklist for Developing AAA Tasks

The following list of activities is a sample AAA survey to begin your staff and volunteer leadership discussion about engaging board members and other volunteers in the AAA program. You can set up the checklist using any software template that accommodates both the checklist and a summary matrix that you can use to track your volunteers' preferred assignments (Appendix B).

I Will be an Ambassador — Making Friends

____ Host a minimum of (#____) lunch/dinner meetings at home ____ or a restaurant ____ .

____ Bring interested friends and acquaintances for a tour of our (facility or other place people can visit). Do this a minimum of (#____) times this year.

____ Bring interested friends and acquaintances to hear a program presentation from staff or an outside speaker.

____ Use my social networking resources to send out our organization's web link with messages encouraging my friends to give and get involved.

____ Share names of those people and funding organizations who share our values and vision, and assist staff and other volunteers with review of these names.

____ Host and/or participate in cultivation events held at our (organization) ____ or at private residences ____ or public venues.

____ Participate in up to (#____) cultivation events this year.

____ Help with special mailings for events and fund drives by adding personal notes to letters prepared by staff.

____ Participate in "thankathons" (telephone calling to thank donors) after fund drives or special events.

____ Become a member of the "gratitude committee" that will organize these thankathons.

____ Participate in implementing strong stewardship practices (ongoing relationship with donors after gifts are made) by making personal visits.

____ Be consistent in writing thank you ____ or occasional update notes ____ , attending donor appreciation events ____ or hosting such events in my home ____ .

____ Other Ambassador tasks I am willing to do:

_____

_____

_____

I Will be an Advocate — Making the Case

____ Participate in program-based training about making the case for our organization so I can become a more informed Advocate.

____ Become part of a speakers' bureau and/or offer to give talks to ____ service club or ____ church or ____ community center or at places chosen by the organization.

____ Using my social networking resources, I am willing to send out information on the organization or an issue we are dealing with to my network of friends for the purpose of raising their awareness of our programs.

____ Provide formal advocacy with governmental or other organizations whose understanding of our programs and accomplishments may improve the revenues we receive from them (or prevent further cutbacks).

____ Use my writing, editing and/or marketing skills to help us create/revise/rework our development and marketing materials and make sure that our messages are consistent across all materials we put out into the community.

____ Participate in strategic conversations about donor cultivation, involvement, solicitation strategies and assist development office or others in enlisting volunteers to help with financial resource development.

____ Participate on the nominating committee (or committee on trustees or board development committee) to create a strategic recruitment plan and/or to assist with the recruitment and enlistment of new board members.

____ Other Advocate tasks I am willing to do:

_____

_____

_____

I Will be an Asker — Making the Ask

____ Initiate conversations with people for the purpose of assessing their interest in making a gift, and then report on those conversations to staff and board leadership.

____ Write personal letters and/or make personal phone calls to invite people to become donor-investors in our organization.

____ Using my social networking resources, I will make direct asks to my social network, encouraging them to give to our organization.

____ Team up with staff or other volunteers to make personal calls on potential and current donors for the purpose of asking for a new or renewed gift.

_____ Chair or participate in committees responsible for major fundraising events, with particular focus on soliciting sponsorships from corporations and foundations using my contacts or contacts provided to me.

_____ Participate in visits to foundations, government agencies or other institutional funders and be prepared to make the case for their new or continued investment in us.

_____ Other Asker tasks I am willing to do:

_____

_____

_____

Remember, this is a starting point, not the end product. The sample survey's purpose is to inspire your thinking about what your organization's survey can look like.

Chapter 7:

AAA IN ACTION — Next Steps

Getting the Board Engaged in AAA

Tailoring the sample checklist to reflect your organizational priorities and your volunteer skills is the next step. Your development or institutional plan will provide most of the tasks, but the brainstorming sessions with board and staff will enrich it, too. One of the ways the sample checklist has evolved over the past few years is through organizations sending me their tailored checklists. They have ideas that I had never thought of.

Be sure the language you use in the checklist is high in "I" — "I will host lunches" "I will make three cultivation calls" and not just a generic list. Having the "I" focus in these surveys heightens the level of commitment.

Before giving the survey to the board, provide them with information about the AAA program and how it is a new way of organizing and managing what many of them are already doing. That will be a relief, as most of them already feel pressure over assignments.

Presenting These Ideas to Your Volunteers

Here is a quick summary of the program that you can present at a board, committee or special meeting. You might want to create a visual presentation of the key points. You have the author's permission as long as the source is attributed.

WHAT IS A 'TRIPLE A BOARD'?

An organization with an AAA Rating is one where every board member is engaged as an Ambassador, Advocate and/or Asker. Volunteers in AAA organizations are asked to sign up for roles and responsibilities they will enjoy doing that will help (name of your organization) increase its visibility in the community and its capacity to engage people in giving and serving.

AMBASSADOR
- Has made a personally significant gift
- A role every board member needs to play
- Has key roles in cultivation of prospective donors and stewardship of continuing donor-investors
- Needs to be well oriented and coached in the message
- Masters of the "elevator speech" (and the "elevator question")
- Catalysts for donor-investor renewal

ADVOCATE
- Has made a personally significant gift
- Is strategic in sharing information informally about our organization
- May advocate on a more formal basis with city officials, foundation officers, another organization with which we are partnering

- Is informed about the case for support and has knowledge of our strategic plan and vision
- Is well coached on desired results of each advocacy opportunity and in handling objections that may arise

ASKER

- Has made a personally significant gift
- Is enthusiastic about the organization and about asking for investment
- Well informed, well trained
- "Matched" with prospective donors (or current donor-investors) for maximum possibility of success
- Teams with another board Asker or staff leader to make calls
- Staff organizes the ask so the Asker's focus can be on the single purpose of getting (or renewing) the gift
- Writes letters, makes phone calls and visits
- Benefits from the work of the Ambassadors and Advocates

This assumes 100% giving by your board members. If you do not have that, you may want to delete (or explain) the first requirement in each role. However, it is difficult to be an enthused Ambassador, Advocate or Asker if the person has not given a personal gift to the organization.

Be ready for lots of questions at the initial presentation about AAA, and be sure that the staff or volunteer presenter is clear and enthusiastic about the program. It will help you have a smooth launch.

Administering the Checklist

At a subsequent board or committee meeting — or after the initial presentation if it is part of a longer retreat — review the AAA role descriptions and invite more questions. Give them time to fill out the survey during the meeting, and be sure they include their name and best contact method (email address/phone number(s)) before they turn it in. If time permits, it is a very motivating exercise to have each board member state two things they have signed up to do.

Before they fill it out, remind them that they can choose tasks from all three roles, from two or from one. In the summary grid (Appendix B) you will note that several of the board members just checked one or more of the basic categories, and did not choose specific tasks. Since then, staff has followed up and worked with them to identify things they will do.

Encourage them to add tasks in the space provided for "other ways I can help" — sometimes board members have a special resource, talent, connection or skill that is not included in the listed tasks. When they have finished identifying what they are willing to do, have them go back over the survey and identify with an asterisk (*) the two or three tasks they would like to start doing first.

What To Do With the Checklists

When the checklists are turned in, let the board know what the next steps are (you may want to add dates after each of these tasks before you put out your own version of this timeline):

1. Staff will review the surveys and prepare a master grid (see Appendix B) showing the various roles/tasks board members have chosen
2. Each board member will receive a letter or email, listing the roles/tasks they have said they would do, and indicating a time when a staff or volunteer leader will be calling

them to help them to review their priority activities and get started

3. When it can be scheduled, a training session in donor development, the basics of philanthropy and fund raising, cultivation, solicitation and stewardship will be conducted: all board members are expected to come, even if they are not planning to be Askers. Those who cannot come will have a special coaching session (the idea of this is usually sufficient to get people to come to the training session — people would rather do this in a group).

4. Materials and ideas needed to fulfill their various roles and tasks will be developed and reviewed and a "Volunteer Tool Kit" created for Ambassadors, Advocates and Askers to use (includes fact sheets, stories, key case points, financial and service information, etc.)

You can add steps that are appropriate to your staffing, timing and circumstances.

Getting the Program Up and Running

Timing is very critical in this process. Don't let this whole program fizzle because you haven't time to follow up with "all those board members." If you are the staff person in charge of AAA, get some help from board leaders if you are feeling swamped. Time the survey administration so it is during a lull in your busy schedule (giving the survey to board members just before your year-end mailing or major fundraising event is not a good idea). Make follow up with board members your priority. Write the follow up letter or email immediately. Let them know when you will be telephoning to arrange a meeting.

If you have 25 board members and there is just one of you, get some help from board leaders in making these calls. At St. Jude Hospital Foundation in Southern California, much of the follow up work was done by volunteers working with the foundation's director. Make room in your schedule for this. Lay out a plan that includes time every day for a week (e.g.) for you and/or another person to do phone follow up with three to five members each day. Set appointments if they are willing to meet; set a longer phone appointment if a meeting is not possible. At the end of the week, it will be done. Once it is done, you will be on your way to getting your AAA volunteer program up and running.

In these phone or personal meetings, begin by thanking them for their thoughtful review and response to the survey/checklist. Go over all the tasks they have signed up for but focus on the priorities they identified. Not everything has to be done at once. Phase the activities over the period of time that matches your strategic or development plan. In that way, neither you nor the volunteer will be overwhelmed. If their activities include cultivation of new prospects, give them copies of your existing cultivation plan including the already-scheduled activities (tours, presentations, open houses, etc.) you have set up. If they are willing to help with board member recruitment, have some candidates ready for them to talk with.

Even if you start with one task per board member, that is a big step forward.

Internalizing AAA

In organizations where AAA has been implemented, it has become the framework for referring to roles and tasks. If you already have board members and other volunteers involved in assignments that are achieving results and keeping them motivated, work the AAA template around what they are already doing.

AAA is also something you can add to your board recruitment matrix. Each AAA role is easy to understand, and the goal of having a good distribution of board members willing to be in these roles is a boost to your recruitment efforts. The summary grid (Appendix B) will reveal the "holes" in your current board composition, and inspire recruitment of people who will round out the AAA on your board.

Chapter 8:

IMPLEMENTING THE AAA PROGRAM — Role of Development Staff

The development office is command central for AAA.

More than just providing a common vocabulary, the AAA grid and individual surveys are very effective management tools for development staff. AAA provides a workable system for following up with board members and other volunteers. Potential assignments are easier to explain within the context of one of the AAA roles, and the continuum of developing a current or prospective donor from curious to committed — so often missed in our frenzied focus on fundraising — becomes increasingly clear.

Development staff needs to be very intentional about the importance of "contact reports" from volunteers. The Action Update (Appendix A) is a great tool — but initially will require discipline and follow up. Post it on a secure website for board members and let them fill it out on line and email it in. If that's not possible, have it in the form of an email you can send out after an event or meeting, and instruct them how to fill out and paste into an email back to you.

Some people prefer to do a "brain dump" by telephone after they have attended an event where they have interacted with potential or current donors. Be ready to take notes when they call. Still others will have to be telephoned by staff or volunteers — whoever makes the phone call should use the Action Update or another form with questions to guide the conversation.

Another job for the development office is to refresh the checklist. While you may only do one annual survey to assess AAA involvement in the overall development program, nothing prevents you from using the AAA list for special efforts — major events, capital initiatives, membership drives, etc. However you use the template, keep it current. Remove tasks that are no longer a priority; add ones that need to be done.

The development office tracks progress and completion of the tasks, so is also responsible for seeing to it that the board chair has information about who has done what since the last meeting. Providing appropriate recognition at board meetings is motivating not only to those who have been doing their assignments, but often to those who have not. Later chapters cover evaluation and recognition in more detail.

Just remember: it is up to the development office to track, nudge, nag, guide and coach board members and to remind your board leadership to celebrate your AAA volunteers.

If your organization does not have a development staff person or team, the coordination of the program can be done very effectively by volunteer leaders.

Chapter 9:

IMPLEMENTING THE AAA PROGRAM — Role of the Board

The **first role of the board** in implementing AAA is to have 100% involvement in one, two or three AAA roles.

Staff support of AAA is not enough: AAA requires board leadership to ensure participation once AAA commitments have been made.

Volunteer management of AAA can be part of the responsibilities of the Committee on Trustees/Directors (or Nominating Committee as it is sometimes known). One of the first steps in integrating AAA into board member recruitment is to have the explanation of AAA either included in or appended to the board member job description.

Another way is to add some prospective board member interview questions that will get them thinking about what they might like to do if they come on the board:

- "What kinds of volunteer experiences have been the ones you enjoyed the most?"
- "Are there fundraising or development activities that are less enjoyable for you?"
- "Tell us about one of your most successful volunteer experiences — what made it work for you?"

You will get some early indications about this person's motivation that will help you enhance their board experience.

In the board orientation, prior to the time new board members fill out the AAA survey, you may want to have veteran volunteers who serve well in their chosen roles of Ambassador, Advocate and Asker tell new board members how AAA works in your organization. Encourage them to share their experiences. Remember that one of the powerful advantages of AAA is that it honors the efforts of those who make friends and/or make the case as well as those who make the ask. At the orientation you can also introduce volunteer/staff teams that are working together to extend the community reach of the organization:

- the volunteer who is a marketing expert and is working with program staff in creating a new brochure and has helped find a printer who offered a discount (Advocate);
- the board member who introduced a program staff person to a person with a large family foundation that is now supporting the expansion of the program (Ambassador); and
- the Asker on the board who encouraged a faculty member to accompany her on a call and watched as a previously resistant donor became engrossed in the faculty member's research and gave the needed funding to continue.

At board or committee meetings, start off the agenda with an "SOS" — Share Our Success. At first, you may have to enlist people to share their stories but, as SOS becomes a regular part of the meeting, you will find that people are eager to share their experiences.

Getting a balance among stories that illustrate Ambassador, Advocate and Asker roles is important at first — but there is no need to have all three represented at every meeting as the program matures. These stories are brief and should include not only success stories but (in spite of the SOS label) stories of efforts that did not work out so well (often told with great humor). Letting other volunteers see that even the most skilled Asker or Advocate or Ambassador occasionally strikes out is a great confidence booster.

The board's role in sustaining AAA is covered in the next chapter. The most important step in engaging the initial participation of the board is to identify and involve a handful of board champions willing to advance the idea with other volunteers. Have them work with development staff to create a successful AAA program.

Chapter 10:

SUSTAINING THE PROGRAM

Volunteer Recognition

Recognition helps sustain motivation. Be sure to find out how a person likes to be recognized. Some like to be publicly identified for their role in bringing in a large gift or doing a major advocacy role. You will have others for whom such recognition is embarrassing and inappropriate.

The best way to find out what kind of recognition a volunteer appreciates is to ask:

- "We are very appreciative of your advocacy in this merger and would like to recognize you for your role in making it possible. We were thinking of mentioning your efforts in our press release — would that be all right with you?"

If the person says no, find out what kind of recognition (if any) they would like. It is far better to find out before making a public announcement. You could end up alienating a valuable volunteer.

Engaging Volunteers in Follow Up

If you find that some board members never have a story to share at board meetings, are avoiding your phone calls, and have obviously not carried out the things they committed to, follow up on it. If you do not, it will devalue the program as yet another idea that came and went.

For busy development staff, keeping tabs on volunteers can fall to the bottom of the "To Do" list. Here is where volunteer leaders play a key role.

Enlist your nominating committee/committee on directors or trustees to help monitor progress. When you receive completed surveys from board members, enlist members of the committee to work with board leadership or staff in making up the survey grid and in developing timelines and strategies for following up. Although staff should generate the assignment letter or email to each board member, be sure to send it out over the signature of the chair of the nominating/committee on directors or trustees. There is no substitute for peer leadership when getting a new program off the ground.

Just as you will keep the number of tasks to a manageable few (for both the volunteer and the person overseeing the volunteer), make sure that you do not overload an already-busy committee chair or member with too much follow up. They will have their own AAA assignments, and will be models and leaders for the others.

Focus on two key areas for your monitoring: recognizing those who are getting their jobs done (thank you calls and notes are great motivators) and prodding those who are not. Too often, we focus on the latter and neglect those who are doing a great job. Remember that high achievers thrive on feedback.

Annual Review With Each Board Member

Another way to keep the program active is to include AAA

---

discussion at the yearly meeting the board chair and CEO have with each board member. If these meetings are not yet part of your board activities, this may be a good time to initiate them.

These meetings have three purposes: 1) thank the board member for his/her service, 2) discuss how the board member wants to be involved in the coming year and identify any constraints or complaints they may have, and 3) ask the board member for an annual (or annual and capital if you are in a campaign) gift. AAA provides a natural platform for discussing point 2, how the board member wants to be involved and what is working/not working.

Using the AAA framework helps keep the conversation focused and gives continuity to assignments. At these meetings, you may find that a board member is ready to take on another role (Asker, e.g.) or you may find that someone who offered to be a formal Advocate for you with a city commission no longer has the time or the contacts to fulfill that role. Let the board member review his or her previous AAA survey during the meeting. It is a great way to get your grid updated, and also provides an easy way to find out what the person wants to do in the coming year.

Keeping Both Motivation Levels Strong
When you focus on keeping board members involved in AAA and renewing their enthusiasm for various roles and tasks, you are able to concentrate a great deal on the kind of activities that keep them immediately motivated: cultivation, outreach, informal or formal advocacy, getting involved in program support.

But be sure you also keep the mission, vision and values — the deep motivation — as part of the conversation. Make sure that at each board meeting there is a "mission moment" during which a member of the community or someone else who has benefited from your services comes in for 10 minutes to say "thank you" to the board. Tie the SOS stories back into the shared values they represent. And connect the gifts and other successes your AAA team achieves to the furtherance of your vision.

For the iPhone, BlackBerry and vibrating mobile phone folks on your board — and for some others whose impatience may be increasingly obvious — balance the SOS and mission moment with an action-oriented board agenda. Forego endless committee reports. Instead, at each meeting, have a lively discussion of at least one key issue confronting your organization or your community. Send more and more of your committee reports as pre-meeting emails requiring action-only response at the board meeting.

Meetings that expand program knowledge, stimulate inquiry and offer new insights into community needs help board members fulfill their AAA roles.

Chapter 11:

ANTICIPATING PROBLEMS WITH AAA — When a Board Member Simply Won't Play

There are board members who prefer to create their own roles.

Frequently they are very busy ("I already serve on six boards and I just don't have that much time to give...") or they have been on your board a long time and already know what they want to do.

In both cases, time will ultimately determine whether or not they want to be part of AAA.

With the person who has six other boards to attend and serve, AAA can turn out to be a good way to manage responsibilities — you can narrow the work you expect from the individual and draw on their time and expertise in a more appropriate way.

For those who have been on the board a long time, it is sometimes an easier hurdle to surmount. When they see others getting involved, and when they see that it is not something in addition to what they have been doing but just a way of organizing and managing tasks they like to do, they will get past their resistance.

If the resistance movement is quietly waged by those who don't want to be categorized, you can work with it and it will solve itself. Sometimes, the real reason is they don't want to be accountable for assignments. A looser structure is more appealing to them.

However, if a board member speaks up or out at meetings about AAA after the board or committee has decided to implement the program, then you have another problem.

They may object that it is taking too much time, that it won't make a difference, or question whether it will work. Handling these questions takes information and conviction, and the conversation should be held privately. The board or committee chair will need to find out what the point of resistance is. When it has been identified ("That's not the way we have done it before and look how successful we've been" or some other reason) you can begin working with the person from that point forward.

The good news is that (so far) there has been no open resistance in the organizations that have implemented this program. But that's not to say that it could not happen with some board members who feel more knowledgeable or have a greater sense of ownership of the past. If you know these people are on your board or committee, the best strategy is to engage them in the formulation of AAA and ask them to be standard bearers for this new approach.

At a minimum, each board member should commit to being an Ambassador. As stated in the beginning pages of this book, any board member unwilling to be an Ambassador probably should not be on your board. The role of Ambassador is simple to learn and execute. If volunteers are unwilling to assume this role, you should find out why. They may have issues with the organization, or they may not understand exactly what the role requires.

Whatever the reason, try to overcome it. Everyone needs to be enrolled if this program is to have the promised impact.

Chapter 12

Applying AAA to Non-Board Volunteer Groups

AAA works not only with the board but with other kinds of volunteer groups in your organization as well.

AAA is particularly well suited to a development committee of the board (often as a starting point before the whole board buys into the AAA idea) and also to committees that oversee major giving programs (e.g., Cornerstone Society, President's Club, etc.). AAA offers an easy division of labor, and a good template for organizing assignments. By balancing the focus of the committee's work on the three interrelated functions of Ambassador, Advocate and Asker, volunteers see how important the work of each is to the other.

AAA conveys to volunteers that the time they spend on the organization's behalf is valued. It helps them understand the development process. They see that they are contributing something important to the cultivation, consciousness raising or stewardship of a donor. Be sure that the leadership of the development or major giving committee is able to articulate the relationship of these activities in such a way that people see their role in achieving the fundraising goal — even if they are not directly asking for money.

If yours is an organization with a Friends Board, Advisory Board, or other non- governing board, AAA can be applied very successfully. Although you may have fewer self-identified Askers because your members were not recruited for that purpose, you will find that the Ambassadors and Advocates enjoy having their roles formalized by AAA. And, while asking may not be part of the job description, there are always opportunities for interested and willing volunteers to be part of an organizational team that visits a foundation to discuss program support, or to help organize successful special events. Those last two tasks can comfortably fit under the umbrella of "Asker."

For committees or for non-governing boards, you can use the same basic process already described: review of the AAA roles, generation of desired tasks by staff, development of a survey adapted to your organization and your circumstances, compilation of the information into a management grid and assignments.

The responsibility for overseeing the activities of volunteer committee members should fall to an appointed AAA subcommittee or, in the case of a Friends' or other advisory board, may, as with a governing board, be part of the responsibilities of the nominating committee.

AAA will become part of the vocabulary of recruitment in any kind of volunteer organization where it is implemented.

CHAPTER 13:

Involving Non-Development Staff in AAA and the Culture of Philanthropy

Although AAA engages volunteers and is managed by development staff, the rest of your staff can benefit from understanding the basics of the program. While it is not necessarily the job of program, financial, administrative or other staff members to raise money, it is very important that they understand the impact of philanthropy and volunteers. They need to be partners in building a culture of philanthropy in your organization.

Ken Blanchard, author of The One Minute Manager, reminds us that receptionists and those who greet people at our organizations are "Directors of First Impressions." It is very hard to build relationships if people are turned away by administrative, program, financial or other staff who treat them with disinterest or disrespect.

- The culture of philanthropy engages the full development team (all staff, board, other volunteers and satisfied donors).

- The culture of philanthropy is an attitude that guides all relationship-building (with vendors, donors, clients, community members).
- It is a belief in the importance of relationships, and that all interaction with others is about developing those relationships.

A culture of philanthropy grows when all volunteers and all staff (not just development) grow comfortable with these ideas and with the relationship-building process and its impact on long term resource development.

We have to build strong board/volunteer/staff partnerships. Because donor development and fundraising are conducted to increase financial resources to support program development and implementation, it is important to get all staff aware of the strategies and benefits of AAA.

At one of the public television stations that implemented AAA, a full staff meeting was held to discuss the culture of philanthropy, the board and fundraising committee's commitment to AAA roles, and how each staff person could help accelerate the growth of relationships that would lead to increased financial and volunteer resources.

The meeting was structured not as a presentation by development staff, but as a forum: staff members who had successfully worked with development staff, volunteers and community members in partnerships to increase the financial support for their programs offered their experience and wisdom to others. It was eye-opening for other staff members to see that their colleagues in production, member services, engineering or field work had grown comfortable with principles of philanthropy and relationship development and were already achieving results.

Here is a sample agenda for such a meeting:

Sample Template
Staff Meeting for Introducing the Culture of Philanthropy
May Also be Used for Board Meetings

Annotated Agenda
1. Welcome and overview (why we are having this meeting)
   a. Defining the culture of philanthropy, how the culture of philanthropy benefits the organization (people feel more connected, valued, engaged)
2. The role of the board (even if this is a staff meeting) in the culture of philanthropy
3. The role of staff (even if this is a board meeting) in the culture of philanthropy
   a. Prior to this session, identify and meet with staff people who have had success as "connectors"
   b. It is critical that they help plan the meeting, and be the "lead-off" speakers sharing their successes
4. Discussion of roles of staff and what it takes to fulfill the roles (building off the previous speakers)
   a. Connectors with volunteers, community, donors
   b. Knowing the "elevator speech" and the "elevator question" (see Session #1 materials)
   c. Responsible for conveying information to administrative, development and/or volunteer leadership when they connect with people in the community who might want to know more

d. "Directors of First Impressions" — Ken Blanchard's theory about people who greet or answer phones in our organizations
5. Making it Happen
   a. Commitments they will make (this can be open ended, or a checklist like the AAA survey, but for staff)
   b. Tools you can provide (Action Update Form — see Appendix A)
6. Thanks and adjournment

AAA can help bring down the barriers between the development office and the rest of the organization. Too often fundraising efforts are separated from the rest of the organization's activities. AAA offers a new way to look at the whole process of philanthropic outreach and involvement.

The ongoing renewal of tasks for the AAA checklist, while a responsibility of the development office, is a great opportunity for board/volunteer/staff partnerships to solidify. Thinking of ways volunteers can reinforce presence, contacts, visibility and impact in the community can involve a much larger group of staff members than previously were involved. It can also keep board members closer to the program side of the organization, increasing their deeper motivations for involvement.

Putting AAA roles on the discussion agenda for a general all-staff meeting can generate some exciting new ways for board members to be involved. Ask all staff members to think of ways that the engagement of volunteers on their behalf would make their work easier or increase its impact. You will be encouraged by the ideas that come forth from program, marketing, administrative, finance, or human resources staff. To stimulate their thinking, be sure that all staff have brief biographical profiles of each board member, highlighting their profession, their expertise and what they are interested in doing for your organization.

Ask staff to think of ways to connect with willing volunteers and incorporate some of their department-related tasks into the volunteer opportunities. Non-development staff also need to know how important their interaction is with members of the community. Keep that in mind, and communicate it gently: from faculty members to radiation therapists to accounts payable staff — they can have an impact on the donor relationships we are attempting to create in the community.

Fundraising is about relationships.

All staff can contribute to the creation of a strong sense of caring and the perception of a culture of philanthropy.
Let them know about AAA.

Chapter 14:

EVALUATING AAA — Success Metrics

There are ways to measure the effectiveness of volunteer participation in each of the AAA roles, and of the program overall. This chapter looks at effectiveness for each of the three roles and offers some questions for assessing the value of the program overall.

It's easy to know when an Asker has been effective. It is also fairly easy to know when an Advocate with a formal assignment has been successful. It is more challenging to measure the impact of informal Advocacy or of an Ambassador's work.

One of the major indications that the overall AAA program is working is heightened involvement of all board members. You see the difference it makes when volunteers are engaged in activities that are motivating to them. Greater willingness to fulfill assignments and the initiative shown in completing them are observable but "soft" metrics.

To set up "harder" success metrics, you already have a tool: each person's filled-out survey sheet and the summary grid of what each of them has committed to do. You can use these as part of your AAA feedback and performance assessment. In addition to following up with each of the tasks people have agreed to do, on an individual basis, here are some ways to measure success in each of the roles.

Ambassadors

Ambassador success is probably the hardest to measure. The work of the Ambassadors is often guided by intuition (subconscious intelligence) as is our assessment of how effective the efforts to build relationships have been. The seeds Ambassadors plant may not be harvested for years.

For Ambassadors, those in charge of the AAA (staff and board) should keep track of the number of contacts reported. The simple "Action Update," offered in Appendix A, provides a good record of activity and gives you an overall picture of who is and who is not getting into their role of Ambassador. If you are receiving these reports regularly (Advocates and Askers can also use them), you have a good assessment tool. Depending on the time and enthusiasm of an Ambassador, you may want to set contact goals for each month or quarter. If recognition for work well done is based on the number of contacts made, you will also see a rise in the number of Action Updates you receive. People will want you to know what they are doing.

Engaging an Ambassador to share an SOS story at a board, staff or committee meeting is another way to assess engagement — the Ambassador role ultimately involves not only the quantity of contacts, but the quality as well. When asking Ambassadors to tell a story, ask them to say what their next steps will be (see Action Update) and what they see as the long term potential for that person's involvement in your organization. Their reflections on the meeting(s) will give you good insights not only about the potential investor or volunteer, but also about the way the Ambassador approaches a developing relationship.

Another way to assess an Ambassador's impact is to talk with new donors or volunteers about how they heard about or got involved with your organization. Sometimes an Ambassador is unaware that a contact has a long term effect.

Six months after a dinner at which she was seated next to a devoted donor and board member of a social service agency in a large city, a woman walked into the organization and presented them with a check for $25,000. She said that the conversation with the person, combined with what she heard about the organization during the evening's program, excited her so much that she had spent the last several months checking the organization out. Her informal research had reinforced the volunteer's stories, and convinced the donor that this was an organization that was a good social investment. Fortunately, she remembered the name of the person she had been seated next to, and a grateful message was delivered with a dozen roses to that board member the next day.

The way an Ambassador works with Advocates and Askers is another measure of their effectiveness. Those who are willing to pass along information from their conversations to those who may be working on recruiting the person for the board (Advocate) or developing a cultivation program working towards a gift (Asker) are not only good Ambassadors, they are good team players.

The overall evaluation of the Ambassador program is simple:
- Are you creating, nurturing and sustaining more relationships?
- Is your cultivation program more robust than ever?
- Are people initiating relationships and bringing people to your organization?

- Is your stewardship program gaining such traction that you are seeing an increase in the number of donors who not only renew but increase their gifts?

Advocates

The effectiveness of formal Advocacy is relatively easy to measure.

On a much-delayed project in a major city, the attention of the planning commission was finally gained by the persistent presence of representatives from the organization whose permits were stuck in red tape. Their advocacy impressed the commission members, and the permit was moved forward. Ironically, just their presence worked: they did not have to speak on behalf of the organization.

The Advocate who is asked to make your case before the planning commission or city council or to an organization with which you want closer collaboration, will give you a report. Furthermore, there will be a vote, or a movement to the next step of the collaboration, and the impact of the advocacy will be known. That makes it easy to give encouraging feedback and to measure how effective the Advocate has been.

The Advocate who participates in your speakers' bureau increases your visibility and presence in the community. Those who lead or serve your committee on trustees are one-on-one Advocates as they make the case to community leaders to serve on your board.

Informal advocacy is a bit harder to measure. The Advocate may be asked to "sound out" someone about possible board membership or their perception of the organization following a difficult period in the organization's history. Or you may want the Advocate to be a "connector," bringing someone they know into strategic contact with the Executive Director or board chair for a precise purpose.

While much more than the Advocate's initial effort goes into the ultimate success of the conversation or the connection, the effectiveness of the advocacy is measured in the completion of the task. Like the Ambassador, the work of the informal Advocate may not be realized for months or years. Like Ambassadors, evaluate informal Advocates on the contacts they make. Encourage them to report in, and give them appropriate recognition.

Overall, the effectiveness of your Advocates can be seen in:
- Wider recognition for your organization and its programs,
- More strategic board recruitment and enlistment, and
- More effective results in your outreach or action efforts.

Askers

Recognize the work of the Asker who meets with, telephones or writes to a potential new or renewed donor — whether the gift is given or not. No one bats 1000 when it comes to successful solicitations, and the effort is in the asking. Askers quickly lose their enthusiasm if they are only acknowledged when the solicitation is successful.

Measure the Asker's effectiveness by completed calls or assignments, not just by the money they have brought in. Remember that the purpose of all donor engagement is to build the relationship — and the asker plays a key role in cementing the relationship with the donor. Even if the call does not result in a gift, or brings in a smaller-than-anticipated gift, the interaction will still help advance the relationship.

And when acknowledging Askers for their success in bringing in a large gift, you should also recognize the Ambassador who may have initiated the relationship and/or the Advocate who may have delivered strategic information at the right time.

Assessing the AAA Program Overall

One of the early adopter public television stations used the following questions to frame an effectiveness discussion at their yearly board retreat after implementing AAA for one year:

1. How have the three assignments — Ambassadors, Advocates, Askers — worked together to improve the overall outreach and fundraising efforts of the station?

2. How has the clarity of function increased the involvement of board members in their "confidence zone?"

3. Are there instances where board members, perhaps unsure of their ability or skill at raising money, have in fact "brokered" a funding relationship between a prospect and the station by fulfilling the Ambassador or Advocate role (the law of unintended consequences)?

4. What "tools" are needed by each/all of the three groups in order to be more effective?

5. What aspects of the program have worked well?

6. What aspects need to be tweaked or fine tuned for the program to work successfully?

7. Are there ways to expand the program (e.g., another station is using the AAA with its Cornerstone Council — the volunteers who cultivate, solicit and steward annual gifts of $1000+)?

8. Are we using the AAA as a complement to the board recruitment matrix, seeking not only the demographic/professional/ geographic/etc. representation, but

also capable Advocates and Askers and potentially strong Ambassadors?

9. Are all board members taking their Ambassador role seriously?
10. How could we make AAA more effective relative to getting information back to the station when you meet someone with an interest in learning more?

As you implement AAA, continue to ask such questions — ongoing assessment of the AAA program keeps it vital.

CHAPTER 15:

AAA AT WORK — What Early Adopters Have Experienced

Since I began presenting **AAA** at conferences several years ago and have watched its implementation at public television stations, hospital foundations and other organizations, the program has evolved. Here are some of the things I have observed:

- AAA comes as great relief to an increasing number of board members who are worried they are being recruited to "fund raising" boards. With AAA, they see opportunities to exercise their experience and skills in advocacy, relationship building, outreach and stewardship.
- AAA has been a powerful tool for helping non-development staff understand what professional development is all about and the important roles that board members play in enhancing the organization's resources and reputation.

- The "unintended consequences" have included not only the previously-mentioned willingness of Ambassadors and Advocates to become Askers, but also the pride and satisfaction that those who simply cannot or will not ask have with the roles they have chosen to play.
- By delineating the roles — particularly Ambassadors and Advocates — there is a clearer understanding by staff and board about the steps in the development process. AAA has become an educational tool for explaining the cultivation and stewardship processes — surely a long-term benefit of the program.
- Volunteers and staff who are engaged in Ambassador and Advocate activities — even when there is still a scarcity of Askers on the board — make it possible for development staff to make asks that no longer feel like cold calls. This has been an enormous boost for them.

There are organizations that have implemented AAA whose stories I have not heard. Often I am unaware that this idea has taken hold during a presentation I have made, and I am delighted and gratified to find out later that it has been developed, implemented and is working in increasing numbers of organizations.

Chapter 16:

IF THE PROGRAM FALTERS — How to Fix It

AAA should be a flexible framework, not a locked-down process that becomes tedious and annoying. My belief that systems liberate applies to AAA.

It is a process for organizing, with a common vocabulary, self-selected but needed tasks that are motivating to board members, non-board volunteers and, in some organizations, non-development staff.

It is a system for freeing board members from the notion that they have to ask directly for money if that is not something they can or want to do.

It is a program that, when embraced by staff and board in partnership and used to help create a culture of philanthropy, can take your organization to a new level of relationship development.

It is <u>not</u> a program for putting people into silos or labeling them with one role or another. Your goal is to move people among the roles, and, if they choose, to grow them into increasing comfort with asking. At St. Jude's Hospital Foundation, that was one of their most profound results: as people's engagement increased through roles they were motivated to choose, their comfort with the asking process also increased. Several who had said they could not or would not ask have evolved into confident Askers by enjoying success as Ambassadors or Advocates.

But if AAA becomes a burden, and if staff begin to see it as an add-on to their work rather than a way of organizing their work more effectively, then something is wrong with the implementation.

AAA should be a path to increased success, not a roadblock. It should be motivating to development staff and volunteers. If the AAA program begins to fade as a priority for board recruitment, if it is not being used as a common template for getting board and staff involved appropriately in relationship development, and if there is a downgrading of its leverage relative to raising the level of involvement in philanthropy throughout your organization, then here are some things you can do:

- Sit down with the nay-sayers and find out what it is about the program that has turned them off;
- Re-state the purposes of the program at a board, committee, all staff or other meeting — and describe some successes that are attributable to the program;
- Evaluate how you are recognizing, rewarding and continuing to motivate participants: was it a big launch with poor continued encouragement?
- Assess the culture of philanthropy in your

organization: if the environment of the whole organization does not support the kind of involvement AAA can produce, then it will stifle the program — in that case, work with those who help set your culture, and ask them to become stronger supporters of AAA and its potential impact;

- Make sure the stress point isn't with the development office — subtle or cynical comments like "This is too much work" or "We really don't need this" will affect the response of volunteers who might like to be involved;
- Do some objective assessment of the benefits you have reaped from the program and weigh those against the voiced concerns of those who are doubting its impact. Then champion your results or offer strategies for making the program work better.

AAA is not an overnight program. It will take time. Give it that time, and patience, but don't neglect it.

Like volunteers and donors, it needs attention to flourish.

As this book is published, the global economy has been in a nosedive and philanthropy is feeling the squeeze. I cannot imagine a more perfect time to be putting together a AAA board — and staff. Because fundraising is not about money, but about relationships, it is more critical than ever to engage everyone in the relationship-building business. To involve volunteers in assignments and goals that are highly motivating to them will keep them on-task and excited about their work with you. Their loyalty and initiative will grow, and their willingness to work on specific tasks will flourish.

Our donor-investors are feeling the crunch in their financial investment portfolios — and what we must do is send out an army of Ambassadors, Advocates and Askers to these donors to ignite their sense of the future: we must be outstanding stewards and let them know about the extraordinary return on investment they have created in their social investment portfolio. Let your AAA team tell your donors that their investments in philanthropy have changed lives, enriched communities, solved chronic problems, addressed crises and lifted society into new areas of potential achievement. When they see the impact of their social investment, they will — when time and the economy are right — re-invest in our organizations.

The roles that each of us must play to ensure the future of philanthropy — perhaps in a vastly changed sector and economy — gain new importance as we consider the importance of maintaining our relationships with our donor-investors while these transitions are made. Some observers of our sector are predicting that one-fourth to one-third of the 1.6 million non-profits will either go under or merge in the next several years. Still others are predicting that our sector as we have known it will be altered substantially in its governance, structure and perception.

If there were no change, there would be no butterflies. Girding your organization for the future means exploring potential changes and initiating them if it appears that your mission will be better served by repurposing or "revisioning" your organization. As a AAA organization — with a prevalent culture of philanthropy that understands that none of this is about our organizations — it is about our communities — we are more nimble, resilient and integrated in our function and outlook.

Our organizations exist because there are human and societal needs that must be met in our communities. From this material, I hope that you will be inspired to devise a productive AAA system for organizing and managing your development tasks for maximum involvement and maximum results.

Kay Sprinkel Grace

Appendices

Action Update

Today's Date: _____

Volunteer's Name: _____

Person I Talked With: _____

Date of Action: _____

What Happened: _____
_____
_____
_____
_____

What We Should Do Next: _____
_____
_____
_____

By When: _____

Comments: _____
_____
_____
_____
_____
_____

Please email or fax this form to: _____

Task Summary Grid

BOARD MEMBER ( ) = staff assignment	ROLES	AMBASSADOR Identify Prospects	Invite Guests	Steward	Other	ADVOCATE Host event	Represent OPB	Cultivate/ Strategize w/staff	Other	ASKER Ask	Other	NOTES
1 Board Member A	AAA	X	X	X			X			X		Notes that "with coaching, willing to participate in the development of relationships with donors as needed where staff think there is a good match and to participate in asks."
2 Board Member B	AAA	X	X			X	X	X		X		Will host event in his home.
3 Board Member C	AAA	X	X			X	X	X		X		Asks that "Dan contact me when I get back to design something for him over the next two years."
4 Board Member D	AAA	X	X				X	X				Willing to work with OPB staff and lobbyist to obtain state funding.
5 Board Member E	AAA	X	X				X	X	X	X		
6 Board Member F	AAA	X				X				X	X	Travels 80% of the time, but would be happy to support in any way given schedule constraints.
7 Board Member G	AAA	X	X	X			X	X		X		
8 Board Member H	AAA	X	X	X		X	X	X		X		
9 Board Member I	AAA	X	X	X		X	X	X		X		
10 Board Member J	AAA	X	X	X		X	X	X		X		
11 Board Member K	AAA	X	X	X			X			X		
12 Board Member L	AAA	X	X	X			X				X	Wants to talk about hosting an event. 'Asker/Other' note refers to willingness to work with legislative leaders for funding.
13 Board Member M	AA	X	X	X		X	X	X				
14 Board Member N	AA	X	X	X		X	X	X				Question mark after X at 'Host OPB event'. Needs follow-up.
15 Board Member O	AA		X	X		X	X			X		
16 Board Member P	AA	X	X				X			X		
17 Board Member Q	AA				X		X	X				'Ambassador/Other' note indicates he's willing to help during pledge weeks.
18 Board Member R	AA							X				Selected Ambassador and Advocate didn't identify specific checklist items.
19 Board Member S	AA			X			X					Selected Ambassador and Advocate didn't identify specific checklist items.
20 Board Member T	AA											Selected Ambassador didn't identify specific checklist items.
21 Board Member U	A						X					

Appendix C

AAA Board/Volunteer Program Survey
Sample Checklist for Developing AAA Tasks

The activities listed on the next few pages is a sample checklist to begin your staff and volunteer leadership discussion about getting board members and other volunteers involved in the AAA program. You can set up the checklist using any software template that accommodates both the checklist and a summary matrix that you can use to track your volunteers' preferred assignments (Appendix B).

I Will be an Ambassador — Making Friends

____ Host a minimum of (#____) lunch/dinner meetings at home ____ or a restaurant ____.

____ Bring interested friends and acquaintances for a tour of our (facility or other place people can visit). Do this a minimum of (#____) times this year.

____ Bring interested friends and acquaintances to hear a program presentation from staff or an outside speaker.

____ Use my social networking resources to send out our organization's web link with messages encouraging my friends to give and get involved.

____ Share names of those people and funding organizations who share our values and vision, and assist staff and other volunteers with review of these names.

____ Host and/or participate in cultivation events held at our (organization) ____ or at private residences ____ or public venues.

____ Participate in up to (#____) cultivation events this year.

____ Help with special mailings for events and fund drives by adding personal notes to letters prepared by staff.

____ Participate in "thankathons" (telephone calling to thank donors) after fund drives or special events.

____ Become a member of the "gratitude committee" that will organize these thankathons.

____ Participate in implementing strong stewardship practices (ongoing relationship with donors after gifts are made) by making personal visits.

____ Be consistent in writing thank you ____ or occasional update notes ____, attending donor appreciation events ____ or hosting such events in my home ____.

____ Other Ambassador tasks I am willing to do:

_____

_____

_____

I Will be an Advocate — Making the Case

____ Participate in program-based training about making the case for our organization so I can become a more informed Advocate.

____ Become part of a speakers' bureau and/or offer to give talks to ____ service club or ____ church or ____ community center or ____ at places chosen by the organization.

____ Using my social networking resources, I am willing to send out information on the organization or an issue we are dealing with to my network of friends for the purpose of raising their awareness of our programs.

____ Provide formal advocacy with governmental or other organizations whose understanding of our programs and accomplishments may improve the revenues we receive from them (or prevent further cutbacks).

____ Use my writing, editing and/or marketing skills to help us create/revise/rework our development and marketing materials and make sure that our messages are consistent across all materials we put out into the community.

____ Participate in strategic conversations about donor cultivation, involvement, solicitation strategies and assist development office or others in enlisting volunteers to help with financial resource development.

____ Participate on the nominating committee (or committee on trustees or board development committee) to create a strategic recruitment plan and/or to assist with the recruitment and enlistment of new board members.

____ Other Advocate tasks I am willing to do:

_____

_____

_____

I Will be an Asker — Making the Ask

_____ Initiate conversations with people for the purpose of assessing their interest in making a gift, and then report on those conversations to staff and board leadership.

_____ Write personal letters and/or make personal phone calls to invite people to become donor-investors in our organization.

_____ Using my social networking resources, I will make direct asks to my social network, encouraging them to give to our organization.

_____ Team up with staff or other volunteers to make personal calls on potential and current donors for the purpose of asking for a new or renewed gift.

_____ Chair or participate in committees responsible for major fundraising events, with particular focus on soliciting sponsorships from corporations and foundations using my contacts or contacts provided to me.

_____ Participate in visits to foundations, government agencies or other institutional funders and be prepared to make the case for their new or continued investment in us.

_____ Other Asker tasks I am willing to do:

_____

_____

_____

About the Author

Kay Sprinkel Grace, CFRE, is a San Francisco-based organizational consultant, providing workshops and consultation to local, regional, national and international organizations in strategic development planning, case and board development, staff development, and other issues related to leadership of the fund raising process. Recent clients (2007–2009) include: San Francisco Museum of Modern Art; Internews; LinkTV; KQED; Kronos Quartet; Family Violence Prevention Fund; Sutter Health Foundations; St. Joseph Health System Foundations; California Council of Land Trusts; St. Dominic's Church, San Francisco; Boys & Girls Clubs of the Peninsula; Loma Linda University and Medical Center. From March 2004 to June 2007 she was principal external consultant to the Corporation for Public Broadcasting's Major Giving Initiative. 110 public television licensees participated in the program which included the development and delivery of webinars, on-site consulting, and facilitation of national meetings.

Her B.A. (Communications-Journalism) and M.A. (Education) are from Stanford University, where she served as the first woman Volunteer Chair of the Stanford Fund. She has received Stanford's highest award for volunteer service, the Gold Spike, as well as their Associates' Award, Outstanding Achievement Award, Award of Merit and Centennial Medal. She was honored in 2009 with the WAVE Award from GirlSource in San Francisco.

She speaks frequently at regional, national and international conferences including CASE, AFP, AHP and DMA. In recent years she has been a featured presenter at the Fundraising Institute Australia, the Swedish Fundraising Council and the International Fund Raising Conference in The Netherlands. In 2007 she organized and co-presented the first seminar on philanthropy for NGOs working to create civil society in the former Soviet Republic of Georgia, and in 2008 she participated in the first Fundraising Festival in Prague and was a presenter an NGO conference in Moscow. In 2008 she presented National Philanthropy Day programs for chapters in Ohio, Texas and California, and delivered programs at AHP/Chicago and other professional conferences including

Independent Schools Association of the Southwest (ISAS), California Council of Land Trusts, Big 12 Development Conference, and IFC in The Netherlands. In 2009 she has presented at the IFF in Prague, Craiglist Foundation Bootcamp, Bridge Conference, and others. She was honored as "Outstanding Fund Raising Executive" by the Golden Gate Chapter of the National Society of Fund Raising Executives (now AFP) in 1992.

She is the author of five books. *Beyond Fund Raising: New Strategies for Nonprofit Innovation and Investment* (John P. Wiley, 1997; second edition, 2005); *High Impact Philanthropy: How Donors, Boards, and Nonprofit Organizations Can Transform Communities*, co-author, with Alan Wendroff (John P. Wiley, 2001); *Over Goal! What You Must Know to Excel at Fundraising Today* (Emerson & Church, 2003 and 2006); *The Ultimate Board Member's Book* (Emerson & Church, 2003 and 2008); *Fundraising Mistakes That Bedevil All Boards* (Emerson & Church, 2004 and 2009); and co-author of the booklet, *The Nonprofit Board's Role in Mission, Planning and Evaluation* (Board Source, 2008). She is a regular columnist for the bi-monthly publication, *Contributions* and has contributed chapters to several books including both editions of *Achieving Excellence in Fund Raising* by Henry A. Rosso and Associates (1987 and 2003), *Taking Fund Raising Seriously*, and *Taking Trusteeship Seriously*. This is her sixth book.

She serves on the Advisory Board of the John W. Gardner Center for Youth and Their Communities at Stanford University, on the board of Resource Alliance, Inc., and on the national board of the Alliance of Artists Communities. She previously served on the boards of the Djerassi Resident Artist Program (Woodside, CA), the Women's Philanthropy Institute, and the Advisory Board for the University of San Francisco Institute for Nonprofit Organization Management. She lives in San Francisco and is passionate about philanthropy, writing, travel and her photography.

Learn more at www.kaygrace.org.
Contact Kay at kaysprinkelgrace@aol.com

About Whit Press

SUPPORT FOR THE INDEPENDENT VOICE

Whit Press is a nonprofit publishing organization dedicated to the transformational power of the written word.

Whit Press exists as an oasis to nurture and promote the rich diversity of literary work from women writers, writers from ethnic and social minorities, young writers, and first-time authors.

We also create books that use literature as a tool in support of other nonprofit organizations working toward environmental and social justice.

We are dedicated to producing beautiful books that combine outstanding literary content with design excellence.

Whit Press brings you the best of fiction, creative nonfiction, and poetry from diverse literary voices who do not have easy access to quality publication.

We publish stories of creative discovery, cultural insight, human experience, spiritual exploration, and more.

Please visit our web site www.whitpress.org for our other titles.

Whit Press and the Environment

Whit Press is a member of the Green Press Initiative. We are committed to eliminating the use of paper produced with endangered forest fiber.